NATIONAL GEOGRAPHIC

T0040050

First, Second, Third

Jan Pritchett

Which skier is **first**?

Which cab is **second**?

Which horse is **third**?

Which bicycle is **fourth**?

Which car is fifth?

Which camel is **sixth**?

first

second

third

fourth

fifth

sixth